Crescendo Publishing Presents

Instant Insights on...

BUSINESS

The Art of Selling
to a Woman

Tanya Pluckrose

small guides. BIG IMPACT.

Instant Insights On...
The Art of Selling to a Woman

By Tanya Pluckrose
Copyright © 2016 by Tanya Pluckrose
Cover Design by Melody Hunter

ISBN: 978-1-944177-63-8 (p)
ISBN: 978-1-944177-64-5 (e)

Crescendo Publishing, LLC
300 Carlsbad Village Drive
Ste. 108A, #443
Carlsbad, California 92008-2999

www.CrescendoPublishing.com
GetPublished@CrescendoPublishing.com

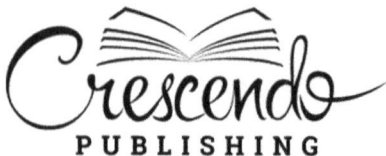

PUBLISHING

What You'll Learn in this Book

The Art of Selling to a Woman is a fresh approach to attracting and retaining the most influential purchasing demographic in the world today - the discerning woman.

In this book, author Tanya Pluckrose takes you on a journey through the three main dimensions that women travel through on their way to making the next purchase - appearance, approach and accountability.

Through her more than 20 years of experience serving the world's diverse elite, Tanya developed her signature *"Surprise and Delight System"*, which creates an environment for her clients to attract and retain their most sought after customers.

In the ***Art of Selling to a Woman***, Tanya provides a step-by-step approach to developing the right service experience for any organization, which results in a dramatic increase of both market share and repeat sales of the new marquee client.

In this book, you'll get ***Instant Insights*** on...

A Gift from the Author

To help you implement the strategies mentioned in this Instant Insights™ book and get the most value from the content, the author has prepared the following bonus gifts we know you will love:

- Her own Surprise & Delight System plan to inspire yours

- A step-by-step worksheet that walks your through the dimensions of creating an exceptional Service Experience, as well as, your Brand Signatures

You can get instant access to these complimentary materials here:

www.tanyapluckrose.com/surprisedelight

Table of Contents

Dedication

To my husband, Michael John Bird, for allowing me to fulfill my life's purpose and passion.

To Jodi Masters, my mentor, visionary, and strategic messaging manager.

To God, my business coach, advisor, and CEO of my life.

To Qantas Airways for instilling in me, over twenty-one years, "The Art of Great Customer Service."

What Women Want
(and Why You Want Them)

"If you want me, it takes more than a wink, more than a drink and more than you think."
– Katy Perry, *If You Can Afford Me*

In the early twentieth century, sales and marketing strategies were developed and refined to continuously capture an increasing amount of disposable income from the marketplace. Most of these strategies were designed to attract men in particular because men were the ones who controlled the wealth and, by extension, the household, entertainment, and luxury purchasing decisions. Institutional training programs, business schools, and "common knowledge" adopted these standard strategies, many of which remain embedded in practice today.

According to Barbara Kleger, author *Marketing to the 55+ Woman* which appeared in Housing Magazine, "over the last few decades, women between the ages of fifty-five and seventy-five have seen their roles change from homemaker to purchaser of security, convenience, and luxury items at an ever-increasing speed".[1] Today, women thirty-five and older make 95 percent of their household purchasing decisions, making *them* the "marquee" customers.

But don't take my word for it. The trend can also be seen in the US Census. According to the 2007 survey,[2] when compared to the previous ten-year period, earnings of the top 500 female corporate officers increased by approximately 250 percent while earnings of females who held CEO positions increased by 650 percent.

---

1   Kleger, Barbara. "Marketing to the 55+ Woman." *50+ Housing Magazine Summer* (2006): 24-30. Print.

2   The 1997 and 2007 Catalyst Census of women corporate officers of top earners; US Census bureau

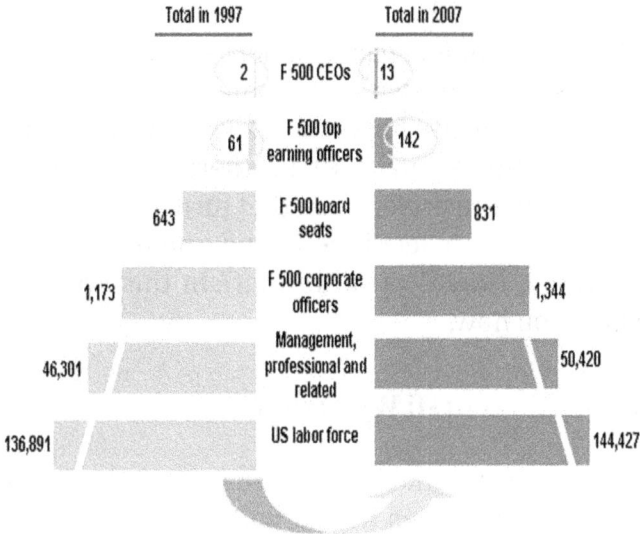

Total in 1997		Total in 2007
2	F 500 CEOs	13
61	F 500 top earning officers	142
643	F 500 board seats	831
1,173	F 500 corporate officers	1,344
46,301	Management, professional and related	50,420
136,891	US labor force	144,427

The Problem

Perhaps then not surprisingly, the majority of female consumers feel misunderstood. Journalist Jennifer Alsever, whose April 2014 article in *Inc.* magazine made the point that too many companies are missing out on the lucrative female market because they still think women will buy any gadget as long as it's pink. Companies too often resort to sexist slogans, painting it pink, or dumbing down features.

The problem is that so many brands and companies continue to use the "tried-and-true marketing standard" developed in another era, and when you tie that to the trend of relying more and more on big data, attempts to attract and retain the female customer are falling short. She's made to feel part of a herd—part of a gross misassumption that all women are generally the same, want the same things, and have the same needs. While it's true there are common standards and preferences that turn most women on, making her feel unique and one of a kind is essential. How do you do that? In this book I'll show you how.

First things first: Who is she?

Before you can understand her, you have to know her. Value her. This begins with the golden rule in the *Art of Selling to a Woman*, which is this: *she is unique, and one of a kind.* In a world that's increasingly converting humanness into related data sets and abstract analysis, it's easy to lose this subtle point—and she can feel it in a heartbeat when you do. The way to genuinely win her heart and pocketbook is to <u>not</u> sell to her. We'll get to that in a minute.

Secondly: Do you value her?

Beyond her unique beauty, intelligence, and intrinsic human value, she's also a very valuable consumer with lots of power and disposable income. Michael Silverstein and Kate Sayre, authors of "The Female Economy," published in the Harvard Business Review, wrote "Women drive the global economy. Globally, they control about $20 trillion in consumer spending, and that figure could climb as high as $28 trillion in the next five years. Their $13 trillion in total yearly earnings could reach $18 trillion in the same period. In aggregate, women represent a growth market bigger than China and India combined—more than twice as big in fact. Given those numbers, it would be foolish to ignore or underestimate the female consumer. And yet many companies do just that—even ones that are confident that they have a winning strategy when it comes to women."[3]

She is also educated. According to an October 2015 report by the US Census Bureau, for the first time in history, women are more likely than men to have a bachelor's degree. In 2014, 29.9 percent of men had a degree while 30.2 percent of women had one, marking the first year that women's college attainment was statistically higher than men's.

She also has money and is influentially responsible for a high percentage of consumer purchases. According to "Women Buy, Women Rule" by Tom Peters (May 2014), women buy:

- 91% of new homes
- 66% of personal computers

---

3   Michael Silverstein and Kate Sayre, *"The Female Economy," Harvard Business Review*

- 92% of vacations
- 80% of health care
- 68% of new cars (influence 90%)
- They also control 89 percent of bank accounts, they make 67 percent of household investment decisions, and they lead 80 percent of DIY major home projects.

She also has specific preferences *unrelated* to price, according to Pam Danziger, president of Unity Marketing:

- She places her highest priority on creating memories—experiences that may or may not have products that go along with them.
- She also expects superior quality and service ... and will pay for it. It makes her *feel special.*

Mark Miller, columnist for Reuters and Huffington Post wrote in a blog about demographic and American women over 50, "...are the healthiest, wealthiest, and most active generation of women in history." These healthy women are ripe for online purchases and ready to enjoy the finer things in life having worked hard for many years.

Let's let that all sink in for a moment.

How to *not* sell to a woman

This book is not about direct selling—sealing the deal with the right statements at the right time in the right manner. The mystery is really very simple and revolves around three major subject areas: Appearance, Approach, and Accountability. I'll train you how to get your A's in order.

There is an art to attracting and retaining discerning female clientele. It is very much like dating a woman, where patience, persistence, and perseverance are practiced with grace. Once you have her "attention and affections," you will win her. You'll keep her for life as long as you remain accountable and connected to her.

Women are the hardest customers to gain, but once you win her over, it will be well worth all the hard work you have put into "courting and charming" her. She will tell all her friends how satisfied and happy she is with your products and services. The best part? You can have as many of her as you can handle, so long as the systems are in place to keep anticipating and meeting her needs.

Your Instant Insights...

- Selling to a woman is not just a process but an art. When you learn this art, you can sell anything to anyone at anytime, anywhere.

- Women make 85 percent of all purchasing decisions.

- Three very key areas in selling to a woman are: Appearance, Approach, and Accountability.

Appearance, Grooming, and Presentation

"Good grooming is integral, and impeccable style is a must. If you don't look the part, no one will want to give you time or money."

– Daymond John

Appearance is very important when it comes to the art of selling to a woman. It incorporates not only the way you groom and present yourself, but also the appearance of your office space, as well as the appearance of being available when she needs a customer experience, which is often more of a collaborative event than not. Are you listening to and engaging with her?

The discerning female's decision-making process begins well before the sales meeting actually takes place. Deloitte conducted an analysis on the differences between the genders and their cognition and consumption patterns. They published a summary of their findings in the Harvard Business Review in September 2013. The main point of their analysis was this: "[Women] are so much more rigorous in the way they explore possibilities and evaluate vendors." [4]

Why appearance = personal experience

Appearance to a woman is everything. She shops with her eyes, and if you personify your business by your presentation—how you look, what your business looks like, how available you are to her in a collaborative way—she will want to buy from you. By "personification," we mean *make the experience individual to her*. When she sees that you take care to make a great, individual presentation that speaks directly to meeting her needs, you'll build trust with her that you will be able to perform the service as proposed. You get only one chance to make a lasting impression.

This lesson was fundamental during my management career with Qantas Airways for

---

4   Benko, Cathy, and Bil Pelster. "*How Women Decide.*" *Harvard Business Review. Harvard Business Publishing*, 07 Oct. 2014.

over twenty-one years. Our grooming had to be immaculate at all times because it was all about creating the perception that if we took great care of our grooming, we took great care of our passengers. A well-kept environment also translates into a *safe* environment.

Recently on a trip with a domestic airline in America, I noticed that each and every cabin crew member had taken it upon themselves to add personal adjustments to the company uniform. There was a total incongruence between the advertising images of this airline's flight attendants and the ones that showed up for work that day. Not one flight attendant represented the well-groomed flight attendant on the prerecorded safety demonstration. The employees' lack of respect for wearing their company uniform to the required standards created a perception that they didn't care about themselves, the customer, or their organization.

Investments in appearance pay dividends

Did you know that Qantas Airways has over 29,000 employees dispersed all over the world? Most are required to adhere to a rigorous standard of dress and presentation. According to Frank Chung, a Consumer Affairs and Finance Reporter in Australia, Qantas Airways reported a record full year profit of $1.53 billion for the year ending June 30, 2016, the best result in the airline's 95 year history. Why? Their continued focus on *and investment* in customer feedback and commitment to providing the best quality product and service. As a result, their domestic and international growth numbers are consistently positive year after year.

Dressing for success does instill confidence in others, confidence that you not only care about yourself, but also that you are serious about taking care of others. Think back to a time when you bought an item of clothing or shoes that were more expensive than you normally buy, and every time you wore those articles, they made you feel like a "million dollars." A feeling of success creates a vibration of success, and this attracts people who want to be around successful people. They want what you have. They can't put their finger on it, but they know that doing business with you will propel them to greater success for themselves.

Have you ever wondered why people don't want to do business with you?

Take a deep breath and take off your defensive armor for just a sec. You may have been wondering up until now why people have shied away from doing business with you. Perhaps your grooming might have something to do with it? Do you honestly represent your brand? How about your work environment, employees/

contractors, or work product? If you are a health and wellness coach, it is imperative you look the part. You can't afford to be cranky or overweight in your appearance because you are sending subliminal messages to potential clients that you don't actually have to give them what you say you do.

I recently attended a local networking event where business cards were exchanged. After the event I was filing my business cards and couldn't find the business card belonging to the woman I sat next to. I looked through the assortment I had, and then it dawned on me: I did in fact have this woman's business card, but the picture on it was of a much younger version of herself. It is so important that you accurately represent your "brand" when doing business. This woman was a business success coach, yet her business card was not congruent with her identity. You must "walk your talk" at all times if you want to attract and retain the discerning female clientele.

There was a time when I visited a prestigious car dealership and the receptionist let the company down terribly with her presentation and grooming. She had no idea that her false eyelashes, brightly colored nail varnish, overdone eye makeup, short miniskirt, and a low, cleavage-revealing top were making a huge impact—and not in the right direction! She did not exude a classy, sophisticated appearance that female customers would find appealing. She made me wonder how trustworthy this dealership would actually be.

Self-evaluation time

It is time now to reflect on appearance. Be brutally honest! There is an old saying that "fortune is in the follow-up." Well, I am saying that "fortune is your grooming and presentation" as well.

Your Instant Insights...

- Women are so much more rigorous in the way they explore possibilities and evaluate vendors. Be collaborative and well presented.

- You must "walk your talk" at all times if you want to attract and retain the discerning female clientele.

- A feeling of success creates a vibration of success, and this attracts people who want to be around successful people.

Appearance Goes Even Deeper

"First impressions are important.
While a book should not be judged by
its cover, many people are unlikely to
read it if the cover is not inviting."

– Anonymous

Appearance doesn't stop with the way you present yourself; it goes much deeper. It includes the way your work environment is presented as well. I remember another great example from back in my late airline days. While on another internal flight within the U.S., not only were the flight attendants' grooming in disarray, but their lack of value on grooming in general overflowed into their work environment. The bathroom I visited was a mess. There was no toilet paper left, the floor was covered in water, and there were no hand towels. This created an impression that this airline truly did not care about its customer service experience. I couldn't wait to get out of there! I bet you can also relate to an experience like this too.

Women love beautiful bathrooms

I was fortunate enough to visit the most divinely kept bathroom at a plastic surgeon's office. The plastic surgeon was a woman who had a keen eye for small details. Her bathroom was designed to appeal to all of a woman's senses. It was conveniently located within her medical suite and was kept smelling fresh and lightly scented. The toilet paper was folded in a triangle, and there were plenty of tissues and cotton hand towels. She had a beautiful bouquet of fresh flowers in the room as well as a few pictures of nature hanging on the walls. The room was dimly lit. She also provided free toothbrushes and toothpaste along with breath mints. She subconsciously let her female clients know that she was a lady of class and sophistication and that she demanded high standards of excellence with great attention to detail. As you can imagine, she was very popular.

In a recent Time magazine article entitled "The Everyday Sexism of Women Waiting in Public Toilet Lines," the author, Soraya Chemaly, points out the long tradition of designing restrooms to meet the needs of men—and women by extension. This is one reason why there's never a line for the men's restroom and always one for the women's. So when a woman experiences a restroom designed specifically for her, she'll be over the moon. It will feel like a special, personal experience. How well does your bathroom meet the unique needs of women?

Clutter and chaos don't sell

A dear friend of mine recently shared how, when she visited a major department store in search of a dress for a special event, she was disgusted by the appearance of the women's clothing floor. She advised me that the whole floor was crammed with too much clothing and that it was hard to search through overburdened racks and disorganized fitting rooms. No one had bothered to clean out the clutter of clothing that had accumulated from the many women shopping and leaving items behind. To top it all off, my friend couldn't find any staff member to help her. She left empty-handed, stating that this particular store was a shopping nightmare, and she wouldn't be returning. (Note how she also told me all about it! Not great PR.)

How to create a buying environment (as opposed to one that *sells*)

In my training seminars, one of the systems that I customize for each client is a *Creating a Buying*

Environment System. It includes the following ten key areas:

1. **Personal**: Have you listened for what she says she needs or is looking for? Anticipating her needs should show up in the work environment.

2. **Relationship**: Are you first focusing on building rapport with her? Your workplace should have a place where you can immediately speak with her in relative privacy and comfort.

3. **Entrance**: From the moment she parks her car, are you making a good impression? I'll never forget the few designated spots near the entrance of a restaurant in Italy marked with a rose (read "*for women only*"). Repeat, I'll <u>NEVER</u> forget that.

4. **Organization:** Are all the areas tidy, uncluttered, and necessary?

5. **Image:** Does your décor, uniforms, messaging, artwork, and displays match your target audience?

6. **Engagement:** Has your staff been adequately trained to appropriately engage with your clientele? Does your displays, interactive video, and/or music appeal to her and draw her in?

7. **Accessibility:** Is your location (physical and virtual) easily accessible? Are you hard to find?

8. **Samples:** Are you providing a sampling of your product or service for her to "try on"?

9. **Anticipating**: Are you anticipating she might be hungry or a bit tired, providing water and other appropriate refreshments at a time *convenient to her*? She's often the last to eat or to rest.

10. **Relevancy:** Are you staying current with trends, a thorough knowledge of your product/services, and what your competitors are doing?

Business environments at home

If you work from home or have an office space, make sure it is inviting and that it is cozy, comfortable, and feels like a living room. Remember 85 percent of all purchasing decisions are made by women, so make sure your work environment meets her needs *first.* Have more potted plants and pictures of family and friends. You want her to feel at home. You are appealing to all her senses. Balance golf trophies and awards with photos of nature and inspiration. This will soothe her and help make her feel more connected to you and your business. Remember the *Art of Selling to a Woman* is a lot like dating; she loves all the attention to detail planned just for *her.*

Your Instant Insights...

- Women love bathrooms specifically designed to meet the needs of all their senses. Make sure yours does too. She won't stop talking about it.

- Keep your appearance and space clean and organized. She should be able to find what she's looking for in your products and services, even if it's just a *feeling*.

- Create a buying environment by anticipating her needs in the ten dimensions listed, not an environment that feels like you are selling to her at every opportunity.

Approach, Your First Impression

"Everyone can be great because anybody can serve. You don't have to have a college degree to serve. You don't have to make your subject and verb agree to serve. You only need a heart full of grace. A soul generated by love."

– Martin Luther King Jr.

When you sell to a woman, you go on a journey with her. Finding *and matching* her rhythm is essential. Too slow, she'll lose interest; too fast, and you'll scare her away. You are taking a trip with her, and while the sale is the destination, the journey is what gets her there. Every woman will have her own rhythm and her own unique set of points of interest where she will want to stop, refresh, and refuel before continuing. Your job is to customize the experience and make it safe and appealing to her. You are creating an attraction and a bond, both of which take time.

Let's begin on our journey to discover the powerful insights that will help attract her to your product or service—and keep her interested.

Are you welcoming?

I am astounded by how many organizations don't realize the power in a welcome. It's a deal breaker because you have one moment to give her that initial warm impression. If you miss it, she'll likely go elsewhere. This moment is all about *her,* not you. You have to take YOU out of the picture and put her in your place. If you want her business, you must make the introduction memorable, genuine, and authentic. The most important thing is to be her friend first and not worry about the sale. If you love helping people, this will come naturally to you. You will want to be of service no matter the circumstances. Helping her meet her needs should be the most important thing to you because she needs to feel you truly care about the need that brought her to you in the first place.

I was thinking of just how easy it is to be of service to her. It costs nothing to have a cheerful attitude. I love being on the receiving end of someone who displays generosity of spirit. Service can come in so many shapes and forms. It can be a listening ear, performing a task, running an errand, offering a compliment, sending a letter of thanks or appreciation, or just being courteous.

What are you whispering?

I love watching *Dog Whisperer* with Cesar Millan because he can quickly tame a savage dog to become submissive based on his vibration of energy. The secret? Every human being carries a vibration of energy, and it's our job to sense it and respond on the same level. Women are very intuitive and will sense quickly if you are being disingenuous or desperate for a sale. Remember back to a time when you were dating. You could sense the desperate ones. They were needy and reeked of desperation. Well, the same applies when it comes to selling to a woman.

One of the worst welcomes I ever received was at a medical spa. The two receptionists did not give me a warm, fuzzy welcome because they were busy chatting with each other while I was filling out the paperwork for the appointment. They made no effort to be discreet with their conversation, the topic of which was in no way appropriate for their work environment. I found it very disrespectful; they made each other more important than me, the paying client. I decided to never go back there again because my first impression was I was not important, and certainly not valued.

The bondage of self

I attend many networking events, and I love listening to how other people introduce themselves. Some of the people I meet make the moment all about them and their line of work, and I usually can't wait to get away. They make me feel captive; they have an urgency within them to try to get my business or referrals from me, rather than coming from a pure place of being of service. Their poverty consciousness comes through time and time again; it feels like there isn't enough. I suspect these people are desperate, and this isn't anything I want to be a part of.

Recently, at a huge conference in Dallas, a woman I met was a perfect example of this experience. She broke all the cardinal rules when it comes to the art of selling to a woman. She happened to have her own booth and was selling a coaching service. Let me set the stage: it was day two, early evening, and the discerning female clientele were winding down with a glass of wine and canapés at a standing table nearby. Instead of sensing the mood and tone of our table (i.e., our vibration or frequency), she approached us with an aggressive sales pitch. She lost us in a heartbeat with her lack of awareness and approach, her bondage of self.

The most powerful approach is to endeavor to become the woman's friend *first*. Don't worry about the sale; it is much more likely to come if you make her feel important and valued first. Show interest in her as a person first before you ask what she does for a living. When you value her as a human being first, you will make her feel good. She will begin to become attracted to you, she'll want to know more about you, and then you can get down to business. There is so much magic in the "small talk"!

Your Instant Insights...

- Make a great first impression by first matching her energy vibration. Find her rhythm and match it. Mirror her.

- Practice being of service to her first. Why is she coming to you in the first place? Make the initial interaction all about her.

- Make sure your staff is trained on appropriate first impressions.

Fortune in Her Chitta Chatta

"So many men think women want money, cars and gifts, but the right woman wants a man's time, effort, passion, honesty, loyalty, smile and him choosing to put her as a priority."

– Charles Orlando

She may be a little nervous or intimidated by the situation. When this happens, she's likely to take a long time to "get to the point." You need to make peace with this. Relax and *listen to her chitta chatta.*

She's likely to ask lots of questions. Be patient with her. Don't interrupt. And just when you think she's finished speaking, count to five before starting. She may make the most of this silence and continue to keep talking. Let all the steam run out of her before embarking on an offer of solutions to her pain and worries.

How to find your patience

In order to stop yourself from interrupting, take notes. You will actually be astounded by how much information there is in the '*chitta chatta*' that you can leverage for the future. This so reminds me of when I was dating. If a man was interested in me on the first date and wanted to see me again, he would verbally give me his whole resume about his likes, dislikes, goals, and values. He would be out to impress me. I would listen carefully to all of this because he would reveal much in his dialogue.

A woman is no different when she goes shopping. She likes to think through her dialogue, so let her. She will announce little nuggets of information that can create wonderful moneymaking opportunities for your future together. You will be able to harness these nuggets to create a strong bond, which is so important to her.

Some of the nuggets of information she may pass on to you in her dialogue will be things like who she is buying for, why she needs it, what her favorite color is, and/or important milestones that may be coming up in the future, such as birthdays, anniversaries, or other celebrations.

You want to make important notes about these because here are nuggets that you can leverage to keep her wanting to stay shopping with you and not your competitor.

How to dance with her when she's not alone

What do you do when she's not alone or, if she's present for the purchase of her gift? A great example was last year when my husband decided to spoil me with a new car. Off we went to the high-end dealership where the agent, a woman, got it all wrong when it came to the art of selling to a woman.

As my husband and I walked into the room, she didn't bother to acknowledge me. She instead focused all her attention on my husband, shaking only his hand and giving only him her card. There was no equal treatment when it came to the introduction. It was all about him. Little did she know that I would have loved being appreciated too, as the ultimate decision maker.

Women prefer more formalities than men, especially when they arrive as a couple. When dealing with a cross-sex or multiparty first impression, make sure you include all parties in the purchase experience. Be sure to ask who the purchase is for – is it for the madam or the sir? Treat all parties with equality.

Where are you looking, and what is your body saying?

Women value eye contact as a sign of respect and connection. The lack of eye contact can make them feel insulted and ignored. They may even wonder if there's something wrong with you, and they may possibly see you as evasive. To gain her trust you must meet her eye to eye, but don't stare or wink, as this will come across as sleazy or a come-on.

Whatever you do, don't look at your cell phone, around the room, out the window, or beyond her when she is speaking. You must at all costs remind yourself that this is a very precious moment, that it's her *and not you*. Find your patience. Get into the present moment and stay focused on what she is truly saying. She will appreciate the undivided attention so very much.

If you have a woman seated at your desk, do not lean back and cup your hands behind your head or lean forward and rest your chin on your hand. No crossed arms, rocking back and forth in your chair, or tapping a pen on the table. All these gestures can be perceived as forms of arrogance and impatience, sending messages that she really doesn't know what she wants and you know better. Get out of your own head and focus on her. She is the Queen Bee, and if you want the sale along with an incredibly long future (read "repeat customer and referring evangelist"), you'd better go that extra mile.

Remember that a powerful way to let her know you are present is to mirror her body language. If she leans forward, you lean forward. If she crosses her arms a certain way, you cross your arms that way.

Who has center stage?

Allow her to be and remain the center of attention. If you are with your children, who gets to speak more? If you are in the company of your boss, who is allowed to talk more? Women accept these conditions in their lives, but not if they are in the process of making a purchase.

Let her speak as much as she needs to in the beginning. If you do need to talk, speak only in short bursts. Let her define what she wants. Don't take over. This may be incredibly hard for you because so many of us are hardwired to fix things. If we hear a problem, we immediately want to go in and fix it. You need to continuously remind yourself that you are going to try to do it differently this time. You are dealing with a woman customer who can offer far more benefits to you and your organization if you sell to her correctly the first time.

Your Instant Insights...

- Relax and make peace with the woman's "*chitta chatta.*"

- Practice strategies to focus on her: take notes and find all the nuggets you can leverage in the future.

- Make eye contact and use body language that is focused on her and that matches her energy vibration (i.e., mirror her body language).

Let Her Feelings Guide the Purchase

"She wanted something else, something different, something more. Passion and romance, perhaps, or maybe quiet conversations in candlelit rooms, or perhaps something as simple as not being second!"

– The Notebook

A woman thinks through her spoken word and shops with her feelings. Her purchasing style is very different from a man's as she is far more emotional when it comes to purchasing a product or service. My approach to purchasing an item drives my husband mad! He can't understand why it takes so long for me to make up my mind about a purchase. He is very transactional oriented, and for me, it is about feeling my way through the purchasing process.

Learning to "feel" your way through the *selling process*

It cannot be said enough: you are not selling—you are bonding with your female customers. Make sure you display to her through your body language that you are truly listening to her: maintain eye contact, nod your head in agreement, raise your eyebrows, and smile.

Remember that selling to a woman is all about building a relationship with her first. She doesn't mind paying top dollar. As long as she feels she can trust you, the sale is secondary to her.

Learning to engage authentically—for her benefit *and yours*

- Note-taking: As mentioned previously, taking notes is very useful because there is SO much information in the dialogue if you pay attention to it. Remembering what you learn, on the other hand, is crucial when creating emotional connectivity. Hear her need(s), offer a solution to the need(s), then seal the deal through the benefits you offer through your products and/or services. The two-for-one benefit of note-taking also helps you remain focused on *her* when you feel your attention span waning.

- <u>Asking relevant questions</u>: In order to truly understand her and her needs, make sure you ask open-ended questions that help create rapport: "Let me make sure I understand you fully ..." or "Are you saying ..." or "It sounds like you are concerned with ..." At this stage of the game, it is not about offering her solutions via your products or services. You are focusing on being of service; you are still allowing her center stage. Gather as much information as possible from her before announcing how you can help her. By waiting, you can be more powerful in your approach to attract her with how you can help her.

Learning flexibility by allowing her to set the pace of the sale

Women take their time shopping. They don't like to rush into things, especially if it is a big-ticket item with a huge expense attached to it. As I mentioned earlier, she likes to think through her thoughts and collaborate with others before making a decision.

One of the worst selling processes I went through was with a success coach. She had no idea that it was important to be patient with me. Her approach was rather aggressive, and it turned me off her terribly. I told her I needed to think about it, and she did not listen to me or dignify my request in anyway. Every other day she kept ringing me up to see if I had made up my mind. I said I wasn't sure and needed more time. She had no patience and even organized a young lady who had worked with her to be a testimonial for her work. This tactic actually drove me away even more. I kept thinking, "Why is she so pushy?" Then out of the blue I got an email through a third party that she had been working unethically for a company. My gut instinct told me that something wasn't right, and she came undone very quickly. Always act with integrity and honesty. If you don't, you will be found out quickly and not only lose face but your reputation in the process.

The hardest statement for sales agents to hear is "I want to think about it." This creates such terror that the sale is over and that you didn't succeed. Instead of seeing it as something terribly bad to hear, celebrate her desire to go and chat about it with others. It will be so refreshing to her—such a different approach—if you encourage her to do this. Before she walks away, highlight the benefits of what you are offering and then surrender. She will be back, but allow her time and space.

Removing threats and deadlines

The worst thing you can do is threaten her with last-minute deadlines or the fact she had better grab it now before it's too late. The discerning female clientele won't mind paying top dollar if she feels she is getting value for her money. If you drop this bomb at the end of your conversation with her, it comes across as cheap, distasteful, and desperate. Maintain your self-esteem, and respect her wishes to think about it. You don't need to devalue what you are offering in order to make a sale.

Think back to the dating world. You loved dating those who were generous with their time, money, and energy. You chose someone who valued you because they valued themselves. Don't lower your standards. Trust that there is plenty for everyone. You don't have to fight for what is truly yours.

A lovely friend reminded me that there are over nine million people in Los Angeles alone, and at least four million would be interested in doing business with me.

Your Instant Insights...

- In this context "selling" is actually bonding; let it unfold at a pace that is comfortable to *her.*

- Engage authentically with note-taking, appropriate body language, and follow-up questions.

- Create a safe space by removing threats and deadlines for purchase.

The Pretty-Woman Syndrome

*"Never be fooled by what you see on
the outside because on the inside
it's often a different story."*

– Author Unknown

A discerning female may wear high heels one day, flip-flops the next

There have been a number of times in my life that I was prejudged in a purchasing situation. In fact, a great example of that was on a visit to an Audi car dealership. As I entered, the two receptionists did not greet me with warmth and kindness; instead, they were cold and unapproachable, looking me up and down as I walked toward them. When I arrived at the reception desk, I asked if I could speak with the general manager. One of the women replied that *he* sees no one—before they asked me who I was or what it was regarding. All they offered was his email address to send an inquiry.

I was taken back. This company's culture created a sales experience that fostered the attitude of judging a book by its cover. The general manager, although absent, sabotaged any sales opportunity because of the people he had representing him and his lack of availability to customers. I could very well have been someone looking to arrange a fleet deal or a mutually beneficial sales relationship, the value of which could easily have been over a million dollars a year. I cannot emphasize enough the importance of effective client qualification.

After a speaking engagement on this topic, a woman in the audience couldn't wait to share about a similar experience she had early on in her career. But there was a twist—she was the stuck-up, poorly trained greeter!

"I was working at a very high-end jewelry store, the one with very identifiable packaging," she said. "It was at their store in San Diego, often frequented by young Silicon Valley executives, cashed up and in possession of black American Express cards."

She went on to convey a story of a young couple who entered the store one evening, wearing casual attire, pushing a baby in a stroller, and holding a toddler by the hand. My friend was the hostess at the door. About fifteen minutes later, the couple stormed out, giving my hostess friend a mouthful along the way. The woman ranted about the fact that they had been totally ignored for nearly fifteen minutes, without a single acknowledgment or greeting, let alone an apology for keeping them waiting. This lady was fuming. She felt judged—so much so that she pulled out her husband's black American Express card and stash of cash. She was incredibly insulted, and you can bet she told all her friends about the terrible experience.

The ideal customer *in progress*

There have been times during the initial stages of my business that I could not afford certain products or services. I had to prioritize where I spent my money.

With regard to services I had purchased in the past from people, our bond allowed me to feel comfortable sharing the reality of my lack of disposable income in that moment. Some were very understanding and incredibly accommodating while others were rather angry that I had rejected them and "wasted their time." Do not take it personally when a woman says she can't afford it—for now. Come from a place of compassion and concern. Be her friend during these hard times, but don't take initiative to get more personal than she already has. If you treat her with respect and kindness now, she will return the favor by either doing business with you in the future or going out of her way to recommend you when the occasion presents itself.

Hardwired to remember negative experiences

According to a recent study conducted by Boston College psychologist Elizabeth Kesinger for the Association for Psychological Science, our brains are hardwired to remember negative memories as a life-saving response. The dramatic details and fatalistic endings are burned into our brains, allowing quick recall when the trigger presents itself again in the future. Although most would say a bad sales or customer service experience isn't "life-threatening," the brain doesn't know that. It just knows you had a bad memory and is more likely to remember it than the positive ones. "You never get a second chance to make a first impression." So remember, in the eyes of a discerning female client, ten good deeds vs. one bad deed could be lethal to your business.

Business Networking and Sex: Not What You Think

The book by the above same name by Ivan Misner goes into great detail about how men and women differ when it comes to giving business referrals. The main point is this: when women receive treatment in a business environment designed to their specific needs, they become far more likely to do viral marketing on your behalf (without even being asked to do so). It's a great read, especially relating to the value of women in networking situations. Although that subject is beyond the scope of this book, I highly recommend you read it as you'll find additional points on the specific needs of women in forming business relationships.

Your Instant Insights...

- Instead of teaching your staff how to "judge," teach them about effective client qualification.

- The discerning female client is more valuable than the immediate sale; she is the value of her entire network.

- A bad sales or customer service memory will live on much longer and deeper in the memory than a good one.

Why You Want to Surprise and Delight Her

"Whatever you do, do it well. Do it so well that when people see you do it they will want to come back and see you do it again and they will want to bring others and show them how well you do what you do."

– Walt Disney

Of your company's future revenue, 80 percent will come from just 20 percent of your existing customers.[5]

_____

5   Lawrence, Alex. *"Five Customer Retention Tips for Entrepreneurs." Forbes Magazine* (2012): n. pag. Web. 01 Nov. 2012.

I feel this is the most important part in the art of selling to a woman. Although it may feel like you are investing a lot of time here, the payoff in the long-term, happy, viral customer will return huge payoffs.

Yet I am astounded by how many business owners and companies think that once they have completed the sale, the courting part of the job is over. Little do they know that the art of selling to the discerning female client has only just begun! If you continue to court her with the same energy and availability, she will continue to do business with you and refer her people to you with more longevity than you've likely ever experienced from your client base before.

One thing that Qantas Airways always taught me was the value of accountability towards customers. If a service failure occurred, it was important that, as the one in charge, I did everything possible to recover that customer in a timely manner with a solution that took the "sting" out of the negative experience. I was then encouraged to surprise and delight the customer with other service offerings to ensure goodwill was restored and the relationship continued to flourish.

The magic of *Surprise & Delight*

For some, *surprising and delighting* may be second nature and come with great ease. For others, it may feel incredibly inconvenient and lacking in the immediate Return On Investment (ROI). In fact, this is why you're able to immediately put her back into your sales pipeline once you close the sale. Because you captured her attention and learned all about her, you have all the information you need to anticipate her next set of needs—and the products or services she may need to buy from you as a result.

The ROI via social media and networks

The second major benefit of continuing to *surprise and delight* is the ROI from her viral marketing. This is often a very powerful ROI business owners fail to fully comprehend. As I mentioned earlier, she loves to collaborate with others and will either sing your praises or defame you, sometimes publicly, through social media. In other words, she will either celebrate you or castrate you!

Many business owners remain under the false assumption that they need to continually search for new clientele as a priority over taking care of the ones they already have. Little do they realize how well their investment in surprising and delighting will pay off in the long run. It's like farming; you plant the seeds and nurture them with what they need, and they give you just what you need.

Creating a *Surprise and Delight system*

How does one go about creating a system of "surprise and delight" in their organization? First, you make the culture shift in the areas we already discussed: appearance in self and the office, paying attention to her at her pace, listening to her, and taking notes so that you can remember what matters to her most. The next step is to actually create a custom system for your organization.

In my workshop I begin this process in two main areas: creating an exceptional service experience and creating brand signatures (mementos). In my downloadable bonus content, I give you an example of both, as well as a step-by-step worksheet that walks you through the dimensions of creating your own Surprise and Delight system.

The system is designed to be both appropriate and effective, using the information you've learned from your customers and the price point of your product and services as its main criteria.

What the absence of "surprise and delight" sounds like

Here are some experiences from a client who just couldn't seem to figure out how to increase sales from her existing clients.

"What words can I use to entice mall visitors to come into my stall?" When I met with this small salon owner, she was spending a lot of mental time trying to figure out how she could increase her overall sales. After reviewing her sales history, it was clear that the best immediate strategy wasn't to try to find new customers; it was to tap into her existing client base. I told her that she didn't need new customers; she just needed to leverage off the ones she already had. When I asked her what her existing clients were likely to need next, she did not have a clue. All she needed was a follow-up system within her business practice to continually connect with her current clientele.

What would a follow-up system look like in her case? I explained that whenever a client visited her salon, she had to listen carefully to the needs, wants and pains of her. This is the time that she puts this existing client back into the sales pipeline. From the relaxed chatter, she was to either take important notes of when certain milestones or anniversaries were coming up or relieve her pain by selling her something from her shop before she left.

If she acted on the information and rang the woman to celebrate her birthday or anniversary or to console her during a crisis she might have been going through, this would surprise and delight her female client. The salon owner would stand out from the rest because of her desire to emotionally connect with this woman. It is all about creating relationships through a woman's feelings. When a woman is appreciated, celebrated, and acknowledged, she will continue to do business with you, even if what you offer isn't exactly what she needs because you do offer value for money by emotionally fulfilling her.

Your Instant Insights...

- Your existing client base should provide 80 percent of your existing revenue.

- Create a *Surprise and Delight* system for your organization to facilitate putting existing clients back into your sales pipeline.

- Your fulfilled female client will sing and post your praises on social media, so don't miss out on this bonus ROI!

Developing Your Customer Experience

*"Kindness is a language which the deaf
can hear and the blind can see."*

– Mark Twain

According Rosetta Consulting's 2014 Customer Engagement Survey, when customers feel cared for, she is "... four times more likely to say [she] "appreciates when this brand reaches out to her," and seven times more likely to "always respond to this brand's promotional offers."[6]

---

6   Consulting, Rosetta. *"Customer Engagement from the Consumer's Perspective."* (2014)

A great customer experience begins with a generosity of spirit

What sort of random acts of kindness could you extend to your female clientele? They don't really need to be random; they just need to *feel random.* These are calculated "client touches" that give her the feeling that she's special to your organization. It can be something as little as a phone call, a text, a note, or an email saying, "You were on my mind. I hope all's well." These could also be a special offer, perhaps something complimentary, or something fun for her and a friend.

At a recent networking event, I noticed that some long-term members were given special access to a conference event through a special entrance. They also received the best seats in the ballroom and were seated first. It's all about thinking outside the box and coming up with ideas, some of which don't even cost you money. TIP: Celebrate her on Facebook with kind words of appreciation. It will be unexpected and you will make her day!

Courtesy is "Kindness in Action"

Courtesy starts with good manners, like saying "please, thank you, and excuse me." But real courtesy involves more thoughtful ways of showing respect. Courtesy is a form of service, which includes how you conduct yourself in the way you address people, greet them, and acknowledge their presence. Ralph Waldo Emerson said it best, "Life is short, but there is always time for courtesy." And Maya Angelou summed it up nicely with her idea that whether or not people remember what we say or do, they will *always* remember how we made them feel.

Punctuality is the cornerstone of a great customer experience

Another form of courtesy is not leaving things to the last minute, like the night before to confirm an appointment or provide a proposal to a female client you are working with. It is up to you to be accountable to her and not the other way around. She is a busy woman and values her time being respected. Martha Beck, American Sociologist once said, "the way we do anything is the way we do everything."

Punctuality is very important to the discerning female clientele. Lack of punctuality shows up when one runs late for an appointment. My militant approach to punctuality came from all the years of working for Qantas Airways: customers have busy lives, people are waiting to meet them at the other end of a flight, or they have to make a connecting flight once they arrive at their destination.

Are you playing games?

If you are, she knows it, and it will hurt you in the end. These games may include some of the well-known tactics that car salesmen use, such as drawing things out until you are hungry, tired, and/or totally out of energy. They can also include the "impending event" close, which implies a set of circumstances may change that is likely to result in you losing the opportunity; or the "porcupine close," which focuses on a high-pressure close *today.* I'm sure most of you have had one or more of these types of sales experiences that likely resulted in a very negative reaction. Oftentimes rapport is built then leveraged, leaving you feeling used and exploited.

One time I received a call from a health-and-wellness practitioner who was also a friend, inquiring about a networking event coming up. This appeared to be the subject of this conversation until the end when she started upselling her new product offerings to me. "By the way ..." was the opening of her sales pitch. To be honest with you, I felt betrayed. I thought she was calling up about another topic and friendship, but instead her agenda was about her needs and not a friendly chat. Beware of sales coaches who suggest these tactics. They don't have longevity. You will work so much harder if you focus on making a sale, rather than truly being of service. Work smarter, not harder.

Are your contracts balanced and thoughtful?

If you are an entrepreneur running your own business, do you have a potential female client sign a contract to work with you? A very successful strategist introduced me to this important form of documentation when I commenced work with her. At first, I was confused and frightened, not sure of her motives. But after discussing the legal document, I realized that it was not something to fear; it was something to be welcomed as it protected not only her interests but mine as well.

This lady was all about being transparent, up-front, and honest from the beginning and letting me know I was going to be safe with any information I passed on to her as the legal document contained a confidentiality clause. She truly had my interests at heart and used the document to create a "safe space" before a lot of trust had been established.

She wanted to set her expectations in writing, make sure I understood them, and that she understood mine. I cannot emphasize enough how this form of accountability actually increased her level of professionalism and made me, the discerning female client, feel safe. It actually built trust instead of taking it away.

Embrace any kind of feedback

Don't be afraid to ask for feedback. We all love confirming feedback, but constructive feedback is the best because it helps us grow and evolve our business to a place where it will continue to grow and harvest lots of fruit.

All large corporations have surveys, some lengthy and some not. I feel you create a great impression about your business by asking people to complete a survey. You subconsciously send messages to your clientele that you care and want to keep pleasing them. You value their feedback. A survey can actually propel your business to another level; it's like masterminding with others in a constructive, confirming manner.

Your Instant Insights...

- Adopt the value at an organizational level that requires a generosity of spirit, including random acts of kindness and good manners at all times.

- Be punctual and don't play "sales" games.

- Ask for and embrace feedback from your clients. This is essential for uncovering your blind spots.

Developing Your Brand Signatures

*"French women know one can go
far with a great haircut, a bottle of
champagne and a divine perfume."*

– Mireille Guiliano

Are you aware that the primary reason clients leave businesses is because of lack of proper customer service? According to a Harvard Business Review article, the average American business loses 50 percent of its clients every five years. Two-thirds of this loss is due to poor customer care. According to the same article what is even more astounding is that 91 percent of small businesses are doing nothing to retain their existing clients.

The easiest way to grow your business is not to lose your clients in the first place. Most businesses ironically invest a huge amount of time, effort and expense in building the initial client relationship and then they let that relationship go unattended, in some cases even losing interest as soon as the sales been made. One way to retain your discerning female clientele is to give away tokens of appreciation called signatures that help her remember you, often. If you give away a gift before, during or after the sale with your brand logo on it she is more than likely going to remember you because of the emotional connection your created with the giveaway. You personalize the buying experience.

A great example of an effective use of brand signatures was the way Qantas Airways used them to create an exceptional customer experience at every level of service, from Economy Class customers, all the way up to their VIP First Class clients. (Note the subtle distinction in how I refer to the different types of clients here—this is also part of the signature mentality.) Brand signatures should make use of every sensory dimension.

For example, in First Class on Qantas Airways, signatures were to offer champagne and canapes, along with specially designed pajamas and a stylish amenity kit. Business Class signatures were an offering of champagne, orange juice, or water prior to takeoff. After takeoff, all sixty-four Business Class passengers were then offered pajamas and an amenity kit, along with a special seat cover to make their space feel a little plusher. Economy cabin had its own signatures too, which included kids' packs for the children prior to takeoff and menus for every Economy passenger.

Another great example was a client of mine in Beverly Hills. He is a plastic surgeon and already had a great sense of how to use signatures to make his female clientele feel unique and special. He did a great job creating a positive, lasting impression around his brand—himself, his service, and his office. From the very first consultation his clients had with him, he ensured that all his patients left with a handwritten thank-you card and a high-end coffee cup with his logo on it, just to say "thank you for visiting me." He was about the exceptional service experience and creating an impression that he was a high-class surgeon with style and sophistication. His approach is heart centered and attracts business from all over the world. Women shoppers love to be spoiled with the little gestures of goodwill and appreciation.

The plastic surgeon's attrition rate is extremely low, and most of his new clients come from referrals. Imagine if you could save a good chunk of your annual marketing budget this way. How much would you be saving? How much could you reduce your overhead?

Another time I attended a farewell dinner that was facilitated by a success coach I had been working with. It was designed to convey gratitude, thanking all her workshop participants for working with her. Not once did I feel that it was a ploy to entice us all to keep working with her. This was her special "thank-you signature"—to create a wonderful lasting memory of our experience with her. She also held a similar gathering at the beginning of our workshop relationship too. Her signatures created the perception that she was a woman you could trust with values of honesty, generosity, safety, and security.

CAUTION: When brand signatures hurt you

On the other hand, poor signature executions can be very detrimental. I often see "cheap" versions (i.e., unthoughtful, perfunctory, and poor quality) of thank-you signatures being delivered that are totally incongruent with the service and price charged for services.

Once it came in the form of a key ring with a logo and contact details on it. The business owner had charged a lot of money for his course, and his parting signature was something I'd throw in the trash; it was not at all what I needed or in line with an item I would use. It was perceived to be on the cheap side, bought in bulk, and lacking class, uniqueness, and sophistication. It undervalued his service offerings and my experience. He would have been better off sending a handwritten thank-you card than a cheap key ring.

Effort should be invested when designing your line of brand signatures to ensure you are representing yourself in the highest form of excellence from beginning to the very end, particularly if you are demanding a high ticket price for your services.

Ask yourself what sort of signatures you could leave with your female clientele. Maybe a handwritten card, a silk scarf, or a celebration gathering? Whatever you choose, make sure it is quality because you want to create the perception that you are about class, style, and sophistication. If you are going to leave a logo on the item, make sure it is in a manner of understated elegance. A woman shopper loves to feel she is part of something exclusive.

A final word on remaining generous after the work is done

Be congruent with your words, deeds, and actions! I once completed a very expensive management course, and the woman selling the course appeared to understand the art of selling to a woman—that is until the very end. In the beginning, she was very careful in her approach by becoming my friend first, being truly interested in me and my life. She appeared to really want to be of service first before the sale.

She had a wonderful Facebook page where she invested in her community with loving words and statements. She appeared to be doing all the right things.

The course itself was very educational and enlightening. It provided a lot of value for the money. The way she undid herself was at the very end of the lengthy course. Her final parting words were distasteful and had disastrous consequences. Instead of finishing off the course with words of continual support, words of greed flowed from her. She advised all her participants that if we were to continue to work with her, she would charge $250 for any additional time she spent communicating with us from then on. What a slap in the face after spending $2,500 on her course! She built a bond with me, and I felt betrayed and used! She lost me as a repeat customer in that moment. In my workshops, we work to design effective transition strategies that put the discerning female client back into your sales pipeline, instead of booting them out. What a huge loss of revenue!

Your Instant Insights...

- Personalize the buying experience with a gift of appreciation.
- Create brand signatures in multiple dimensions of high quality, not necessarily high price.
- Use brand signatures to put your female clients back into your sales pipeline.

Acknowledgements

A heartfelt thank-you goes out to Jodi Masters, CEO of Webvoice, Inc. whose gifts and talents in business and marketing strategy were instrumental to me. It was this brilliant lady who defined my message, pitch, and audience, and then orchestrated it into this masterpiece of a book with its powerful insights and words of wisdom.

Thank you to Qantas Airways for all the wisdom of experience, skills, teachings, and insights that you instilled in me within the wonderful world of customer service.

About the Author

Tanya Pluckrose is an expert and thought leader on the subject of attracting and retaining high-value clientele. Over the last 20 years, Pluckrose has lead teams that addressed the needs of more than 1.3 million diverse VIP customers while safely managing state-of-the-art aircrafts, including the A380 valued in excess of US $375.3M. She's a frequent speaker to growing businesses on the fine art of creating and maintaining brand value.

Through her more than 20 years of experience serving the world's diverse elite, Tanya Pluckrose developed her signature *"Surprise and Delight System"*, which creates an environment for her clients to attract and retain their most sought after customers.

As an award-winning instructor and author of international leadership, customer service and brand management programs for Qantas Airways, Tanya trained and lead more than 10,000 support staff responsible for creating world-class customer experience that is second to none.

Tanya attended the University of Queensland in Australia, and received more than 20 certificates and a diploma in the areas of training, leadership, "creating great," change management, service behaviors, customer service and key performance from TAFE and Qantas College.

Born and raised in South Africa and Hong Kong, she moved to Australia as a young adult. While working traveling the globe for Qantas Airways, she met her husband. They now live by the beach in Southern California.

Connect with the Author

Website:
www.tanyapluckrose.com

Email:
tanya@tanyapluckrose.com

Social Media:

Facebook: www.facebook.com/tanya.pluckrose

LinkedIn: www.linkedin.com/in/Tanya-Pluckrose

Instagram: www.instagram.com/tanyapluckrose

Pinterest: www.pinterest.com/tanpluckrose/

Twitter:@TanyaPluckrose

About Crescendo Publishing

Crescendo Publishing is a boutique-style, concierge VIP publishing company assisting entrepreneurs with writing, publishing, and promoting their books for the purposes of lead-generation and achieving global platform growth, then monetizing it for even more income opportunities.

Check out some of our latest best-selling
AuthorPreneurs at
http://CrescendoPublishing.com/new-authors/

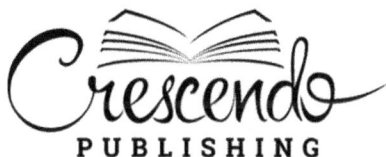

About the Instant Insights™ Book Series

The *Instant Insights™ Book Series* is a fact-only, short-read, book series written by EXPERTS in very specialized categories. These high-value, high-quality books can be produced in ONLY 6-8 weeks, from concept to launch, in BOTH PRINT & eBOOK Formats!

This book series is FOR YOU if:

- You are an expert in your niche or area of specialty

- You want to write a book to position yourself as an expert

- You want YOUR OWN book – NOT a chapter in someone else's book

- You want to have a book to give to people when you're speaking at events or simply networking

- You want to have it available quickly

- You don't have the time to invest in writing a 200-page full book

- You don't have a ton of money to invest in the production of a full book – editing, cover design, interior layout, best-seller promotion

- You don't have a ton of time to invest in finding quality contractors for the production of your book – editing, cover design, interior layout, best-seller promotion

For more information on how you can become an *Instant Insights™* author,
visit www.InstantInsightsBooks.com

More Books in the Instant Insight Series

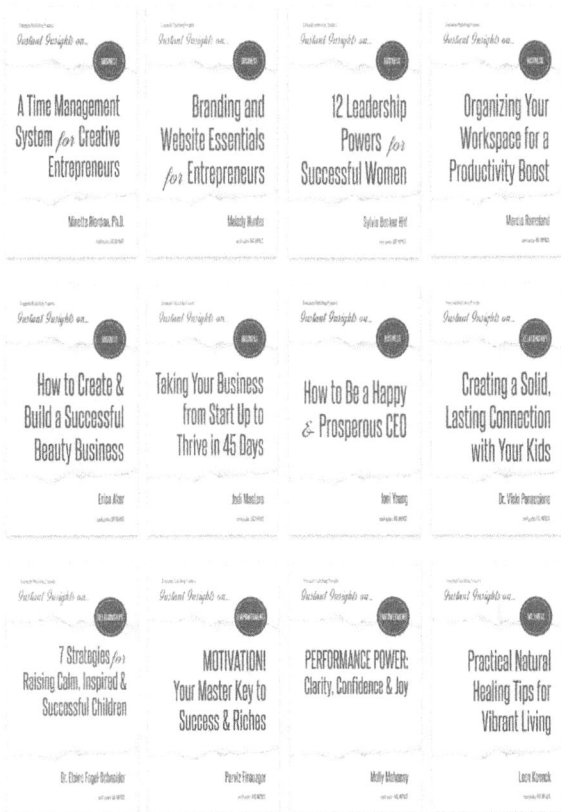

Instant Insights on...
A Time Management System for Creative Entrepreneurs
Mireille Riordan, Ph.D.

Instant Insights on...
Branding and Website Essentials for Entrepreneurs
Melody Hunter

Instant Insights on...
12 Leadership Powers for Successful Women
Sylvia Becker-Hill

Instant Insights on...
Organizing Your Workspace for a Productivity Boost
Monica Ramsland

Instant Insights on...
How to Create & Build a Successful Beauty Business
Erica Alzer

Instant Insights on...
Taking Your Business from Start Up to Thrive in 45 Days
Jodi Mandara

Instant Insights on...
How to Be a Happy & Prosperous CEO
Toni Young

Instant Insights on...
Creating a Solid, Lasting Connection with Your Kids
Dr. Viola Paraschiv

Instant Insights on...
7 Strategies for Raising Calm, Inspired & Successful Children
Dr. Eldene Fogell-Schneider

Instant Insights on...
MOTIVATION! Your Master Key to Success & Riches
Parniz Firouzgar

Instant Insights on...
PERFORMANCE POWER: Clarity, Confidence & Joy
Molly Mahoney

Instant Insights on...
Practical Natural Healing Tips for Vibrant Living
Laura Koczwick

Crescendo
CrescendoPublishing.com